SANTA MARIA PUBLI

j599.3232 BARE, COLLEEN
Cop. 3 CAM STANLEY
TREE SQUIRRELS.
c1983

SANTA MARIA PUBLIC LIBRARY
3 2113 00085 1371

Discarded by
Santa Maria Library

D0579253

ORC JAN 14 '85

OFFICIALLY NOTED
pen marks pg 79
mo/cc 1/09

BRANCH COPY

DEMCO

TREE
SQUIRRELS

TREE SQUIRRELS

Colleen Stanley Bare

Illustrated with photographs by the author

DODD, MEAD & COMPANY · NEW YORK

J
599.3232

Copyright © 1983 by Colleen Stanley Bare
Photographs © 1983 by Colleen Stanley Bare
All rights reserved
No part of this book may be reproduced in any form
without permission in writing from the publisher
Distributed in Canada by
McClelland and Stewart Limited, Toronto
Manufactured in the United States of America
1   2   3   4   5   6   7   8   9   10

Library of Congress Cataloging in Publication Data

Bare, Colleen Stanley.
    Tree squirrels.

    Includes index.   12/84
    Summary: Focuses on the life cycle of the tree
squirrels of North America, including the gray, fox,
tassel-eared, red, and flying squirrels.
    1. Squirrels—North America—Juvenile literature.
2. Mammals—North America—Juvenile literature.
[1. Squirrels]   I. Title.   895
QL737.R68B365   1983   599.32′32   83-8959
ISBN 0-396-08208-4

To Lorraine

CONTENTS

INTRODUCTION

Tree squirrels are very special. They are the acrobats of our forests, racing along branches, leaping from tree to tree. Occasionally, a squirrel will jump onto a spindly limb that bends and sways dangerously. But, it can usually hang on, sometimes upside down. If it *should* fall, the big bushy tail will fan out like a parachute, slowing the squirrel's descent so that it can glide to earth for a safe landing.

They are also high-wire gymnasts and are just as agile running along telephone and power lines as they are in trees. Such skill is usually admired, until a squirrel gnaws on an electrical cable which causes a short circuit, cutting off electricity or telephone

Tree squirrels are at home high in trees.

service for thousands of persons. This has happened in a number of communities where tree squirrels live near people.

But, sometimes, tree squirrels have been honored. The gray squirrel is the state mammal of North Carolina. In Longview, Washington, a sixty-five-foot-long bridge, called "Nutty Narrows," was built just for the town's gray squirrels. It is twenty feet above the ground and spans a busy street, enabling the squirrels to cross safely from the trees on one side to those on the other. When it was first opened in 1963, nuts were placed on the bridge and in feeders at each end to encourage the squirrels to use it. Soon, the busy grays were running back and forth across "Nutty Narrows."

The city of Olney, Illinois, protects and feeds its population of unusual white-colored gray squirrels. They are the town's trademark and are featured on shoulder patches worn on the uniforms of every policeman and fireman. A city ordinance also gives the squirrels the right-of-way on all streets, and anyone hitting a squirrel with an automobile, or caught taking one out of town, is subject to a stiff fine.

People who live with tree squirrels, as pets or to study them, say that they are intelligent. Certainly, they are hard working, resourceful, clever, sometimes cunning, agile, quick, successful, and interesting.

Chapter 1
HISTORY

Tree squirrels have been important in history. The American Indians hunted them with bows and arrows and baited traps, using the meat as a nutritious food and the fur for clothing. The Cherokees called the gray squirrel *saloli*, meaning "squirrel," and thought that people suffering from rheumatism should not eat its meat because of the squirrel's custom of eating in a cramped position. Ojibwa Indians named the red squirrel *adjidamo* which meant, appropriately, "tail-in-air."

When the first settlers arrived on American shores, they found an abundance of both forests and squirrels. There were so many trees that, it is said, a squirrel could cross the country from the Atlantic Ocean to the Mississippi River without touching the ground. The early frontiersmen became very skilled at using rifles

Squirrels eat in a hunched position. This led the Indians to believe that people with rheumatism should not eat squirrel meat.

to shoot wild game for their food, especially the elusive squirrels. Historians claim that it was this marksmanship, gained from squirrel shooting, that contributed to America's defeat of the British in the Revolutionary War. During this period, popular dishes were squirrel pie, squirrel stew, and squirrel and dumplings.

In the late 1700s and into the next century, some of the millions of tree squirrels that roamed the forest lands became trouble-makers. They damaged the settlers' crops which led to squirrel-hunting expeditions by entire communities. Hundreds of thousands of the squirrels were killed until, finally, there was concern over their dwindling numbers. Meanwhile, trees were being felled for lumber, forests were cleared for farming, and much of the squirrel habitat gradually disappeared. By 1900, there was fear that the gray squirrel might actually become extinct. Fortunately, limits were placed on squirrel hunting, which still exist in many states. Today, gray and fox squirrels are important game animals in the United States, and millions are taken by hunters every year, particularly for their pelts.

The tree squirrel almost played a role in the fairy tale *Cinderella*. Apparently, the slippers worn by Cinderella were really made of squirrel fur and not of glass at all. The original story was told in the Norman-French language, and the word

vair, meaning squirrel fur, was used to describe the slippers. By the time the story had been retold many times, this word became verre, which sounds the same but is the French term for glass. Thus, poor Cinderella ended up wearing uncomfortable glass slippers instead of soft, furry squirrel ones.

Chapter 2
KINDS OF SQUIRRELS

Tree squirrels have been on earth for about 28 million years. They are the most common of the some 250 squirrel species in the world, all gnawing-type mammals that scientists have placed in the order Rodentia and in the family called Sciuridae. Within this family, there are three categories of squirrels: ground, tree, and flying. Their main differences are that most ground squirrels live in burrows and hibernate, or take a deep winter sleep. The others live in trees and do not hibernate. This book is about the tree dwellers, including the flying squirrels, of North America.

North American tree squirrels can be divided into three groups, or genera: *Sciurus, Tamiasciurus,* and *Glaucomys.* The largest genus is *Sciurus,* Greek meaning "shade-tail" or "creature that sits in the shadow of its tail," and includes the gray, fox, and tassel-

16

The eastern gray squirrel

eared squirrels. *Tamiasciurus*, from the Greek *tamias* which means "to store" and refers to the animals' food-storing traits, is made up of only the North American red squirrels. Flying squirrels belong to the genus *Glaucomys*, or "gray mouse," so-named because they resemble bushy-tailed, large gray mice.

Of the five kinds of tree-dwelling squirrels in this country, all except the flying squirrel are diurnal, or active only in the daytime. Flying squirrels just come out at night and are nocturnal.

The EASTERN GRAY SQUIRREL (*Sciurus carolinensis*) is the most common squirrel in America and is equally at home in hardwood forests or city parks. Its natural range includes the entire eastern half of the country, from the Atlantic Coast to Texas and from

17

Tree squirrels are often found on college campuses. This eastern gray is at Harvard University.

southern Canada to the Gulf of Mexico. It has also been introduced into some parklands of the Far West. You may have already met this attractive beggar, because it is the popular squirrel of many parks, including New York's Central Park, the Boston Common, Lafayette Park and the White House grounds in Washington, D.C., and Golden Gate Park in San Francisco. It is also present on many college campuses. Weighing about a pound, it is around eighteen inches long, including a nine-inch tail. It molts and gets a new fur coat twice a year, grayish with white underparts in winter and yellow-brownish in summer.

In a few localities, pure black or all-white forms of the eastern gray squirrel are found. The black are called *melanistic*, because they have an excess of melanin, a dark pigment, in their skin and hair. The pink-eyed white squirrels, known as *albinos*, are more rare, because their lack of color pigment makes them very visible to their enemies, and they soon die out. Also, when albinos breed with normally colored gray squirrels, the offspring are usually gray. So, researchers say that a population of white squirrels can only survive in areas where the animals are isolated from other normal gray squirrels and are protected from predators. Such a place is Olney, Illinois, called "the home of the white squirrel," where about seven hundred live and are watched over by the townspeople. Both the city and the state of Illinois have laws pro-

18

The fox squirrel is the largest of our tree squirrels. ⇨

⇨A western gray squirrel

claiming it unlawful for a person to harm a white squirrel at any time.

The WESTERN GRAY SQUIRREL (*Sciurus griseus*) is the Pacific Coast variety of the eastern gray. It is slightly larger, grayer in color, and is found in California, Oregon, and Washington.

The FOX SQUIRREL (*Sciurus niger*) is the largest of our tree squirrels, averaging two pounds and two feet in length, including the tail. It exists in most of the same states as the eastern gray, except that it has become extinct in New England and is moving farther westward into the prairie states. Like the gray, its natural habitat is forests of oak, hickory, maple, and other hardwood trees. It is also the common park and cemetery squirrel of the Midwest and can readily adapt to the presence of human beings. It is seen in a variation of three colors, depending upon where it lives: reddish with light underparts in the eastern portion of its range, gray in the western part, and black to brownish in the South.

The two TASSEL-EARED SQUIRRELS, the Abert's squirrel (*Sciurus aberti*) and its subspecies, the Kaibab squirrel (*Sciurus aberti kaibabensis*), are relatively rare and limited in number. The Kaibab has an especially small range and is found only on the north rim of Arizona's Grand Canyon, in an area forty miles long and twenty miles wide. The Abert's squirrel lives in isolated, high mountain, pine forests to the south of the Grand Canyon in central Arizona, New Mexico, and northern Colorado. Both squirrels are large (twenty inches long, one-and-a-half pounds) and handsome. Their colors range from dark gray to black, with a red-brown band running down the back and tufts of hair growing up from the tips of the ears. The Abert's is white underneath, with a tail that is dark gray above and white below. The Kaibab has dark underparts and a white tail.

The North American RED SQUIRREL (*Tamiasciurus hudsonicus*), also called the chickaree, is the noisiest and the smallest of our tree squirrels. This chatterbox is often referred to as "the sentinel of the forest" because of its scolding and sputtering at intruders. Its voice can be heard in the softwood pine and fir forests of Alaska, Canada, the northeastern and Rocky Mountain states, and as far south as the Carolinas. Only about half the size of a large gray squirrel, it has an average length of one foot and an eight-ounce weight. In color, it is red to grayish-red above, with white underparts and a narrow black line along its sides during the summer. Its ears are more tufted than those of the gray or fox squirrels, especially in winter. The western species of the family is the Douglas squirrel (*Tamiasciurus douglasii*) found in Cali-

The flying squirrel is nocturnal and about the size of a large mouse.

fornia, Oregon, and Washington, and also nicknamed the chickaree. This bundle of energy differs from its eastern counterpart mainly in coat color and is more of an olive red, grayer in winter, with yellow or rust underneath. The North American red squirrel should not be confused with the European red squirrel (*Sciurus vulgaris*), which is of a different genus and species and is common to Great Britain and Europe.

The FLYING SQUIRREL is a tiny squirrel that you rarely see, because it only comes out at night. There are two species in North America, the southern flying squirrel (*Glaucomys volans*) found in hardwood forests in eastern states from the Atlantic Ocean to Mexico, and the northern flying squirrel (*Glaucomys sabrinus*), living in the evergreens of Alaska, Canada, and in northeastern

24

United States and the Far West. Scientists have placed flying squirrels in a different subfamily (Pteromyinae) from the tree squirrels (Sciurinae). Southern and northern flying squirrels look alike, grayish-brown above and white below, with very large eyes and small ears. However, the southern is smaller—nine inches long, weighing two ounces, to the northern's eleven-inch length and five-ounce weight.

A flying squirrel doesn't fly like a bird or jump like a tree squirrel. It has a thin fold of loose skin, covered by fur, that connects its front and hind feet. This skin, also called a membrane, stretches out when it flies, and its whole body becomes a sort of hang glider. It can't soar upward like a bird, so it must take off from the top of a tree or a high limb and glide downward. It is able to cover a distance of one hundred or more feet. Flying squirrels spend their days curled up asleep in tree holes.

All squirrels that live in the trees have practically the same characteristics and lead similar lives. As you learn about what they do, and how they do it, you will see how truly remarkable they are.

Chapter 3
TALL TAILS

The tree squirrel's special trademark is its long, plumelike tail that is half the length of its body. Considered by some to be the most magnificent tail of any wild animal, it certainly is the squirrel's most outstanding characteristic. Among North American tree squirrels, the largest, most abundant tail probably belongs to the western gray, and the most unusual is the pure white one of the rare Kaibab. The small red squirrel has the least impressive tail, being narrower and less fluffy, but it makes up for its size by constant movement, reflecting the energetic personality of its owner.

Squirrel tails are not just for beauty. They are closely involved with the life and safety of the animal, and a tree squirrel with a damaged or severed tail usually cannot survive. This is because

The western gray squirrel has the largest tail.

Squirrel shaded by its tail in the noonday sun. ⇨

The red squirrel has a small tail. ⬎

the tail has so many important uses. The squirrel has excellent control over its tail and can twist it, turn it, and even guide the direction of the hairs within it. On hot days, lying on a limb for a midday rest, the squirrel will curl the tail over its back and head as a sunshade. In the same way, when it rains the tail becomes an umbrella. In cold weather, it serves as a warm blanket, draped around the squirrel in its nest. There are many stories describing the use of the tail as a parachute when squirrels have fallen out of trees or from other high places. One tells of a squirrel that accidentally jumped off a cliff, six hundred feet above the ground.

The tail fanned out, like a parasol, and the squirrel moved its legs as though it were swimming, gently falling to earth for a safe landing.

The tail serves as a balance when the squirrel is climbing, running, and leaping between branches and trees. It also acts as a rudder for changing directions and making quick, sharp turns.

Squirrels use their tails to communicate. When a squirrel is advancing on another, such as two males in the mating season, the attacker will fluff out the hairs on his tail, possibly to make it look larger, and curl the tail high over his back. The fluffing and posturing of the tail is also important during courtship. Angry squirrels do a lot of jerking and flicking of their tails, accompanied by vocal barking, squeaking, and quacking. The feisty red squirrel is adept at this.

Although swimming squirrels do use their tails to help them keep afloat, no one seems to know whether a tail can be used in the manner described in the story *Squirrel Nutkins*. In this Beatrix Potter fable, Squirrel Nutkins floats on a piece of wood, with his tail used as a sail—a possibility as yet unproved.

Squirrels spend a lot of time grooming their tails. The process includes moistening the front paws with their tongues for shampooing the face and neck, licking the body fur, and then holding the tail between the paws for combing with its teeth and

30

tongue washing. When the tail gets into something sticky, such as pitch from a pinecone, the squirrel may spend hours trying to remove it using teeth and claws.

One question remains. Where does the squirrel store its long, bushy tail when it is sitting in a tree? There are several answers. The tail can rest on a limb behind the squirrel, which helps to

31

. . . hang straight down . . .

. . . stand up behind the squirrel's back, against the trunk . . .

. . . stretch out behind in a straight line.

maintain balance. Or, it can hang straight down. It can stand up behind the squirrel's back, often against a tree trunk.

Whatever the situation, the tree squirrel will always find a satisfactory spot for its all-important tail.

34

Chapter 4
SQUIRREL WORLD IN THE TREES

One morning, camera in hand, I was stalking a gray squirrel in the woods. It was bounding along the ground, nosing here, nibbling there, staying well ahead. Suddenly, a coyote stuck its head out through some limbs in a fallen tree, darting back when it saw me. Instantly, the squirrel leaped forward, scurrying straight up a tree trunk, and stopped about halfway. It hung there motionless, for a long minute, until a blue jay gave a loud warning squawk. Up went the squirrel, racing along branches, climbing higher and higher into the treetops. Finally, it made a flying twenty-foot leap into a neighboring tree and disappeared.

Tree squirrels are spectacular climbers. This is how they elude their enemies and can be in such command of the trees. But, how do they do it?

One explanation lies in their large, sturdy feet and powerful legs built for climbing. Each foot has long, slender toes like fingers, four on the front and five on the rear. Every toe has a sharp curving claw that works like a hook against the tree bark, so that the animal can hang on. A squirrel always comes down a tree headfirst, with its hind feet extended out behind the body and its head raised up. It may stop partway down the trunk, hanging for several minutes, frozen, until it is sure there is no danger on

Squirrel-hunting coyote

36

Hanging onto the tree trunk, motionless

A fox squirrel hanging on with its sharp claws.

Squirrels always come down headfirst, with hind feet extended behind the body.

◁

Squirrels have excellent vision, hearing, and sense of smell.

▷

the ground. When a squirrel climbs up a tree, it spreads out its legs, using the front and back feet alternately in pairs. Coming down, each foot is used individually. But, the secret to the squirrel's amazing sense of balance is its big tail. It serves as a balancer and a rudder for climbing and leaping.

Exceptional eyesight is also important. The placement of the

eyes at the sides of the head gives the squirrel a very large field of vision. It can see all around—to each side, behind, and up and down—without moving its head, which helps in running and jumping. It is able to see long distances, one study showing that a squirrel can recognize the identity of another fifty feet away. When it is getting ready to leap, it moves its head up and down to judge the distance. This seems to work, because squirrels usually make perfect landings.

Squirrels have run-around-the-tree-trunk chases with each other, circling around and around as they climb. But, if an intruder comes near, a squirrel will "sidle" or slowly rotate around the tree, so that the trunk is always between the invader and the squirrel.

The squirrel's world revolves around its den or tree house. Here the animals rest and sleep, raise families, hide from predators, and are sheltered from bad weather. From a squirrel's point of view, the ideal tree house is a natural hole high up in a large, older tree. This may be an abandoned woodpecker hole or an existing cavity in a hollow tree trunk. When a squirrel moves in, it becomes a house remodeler. It cleans out rot and litter from the hole and brings in new materials such as leaves, pieces of bark, and twigs to make a soft, dry bed. This kind of nest is commonly occupied by several squirrels at a time and may be used for years by many

41

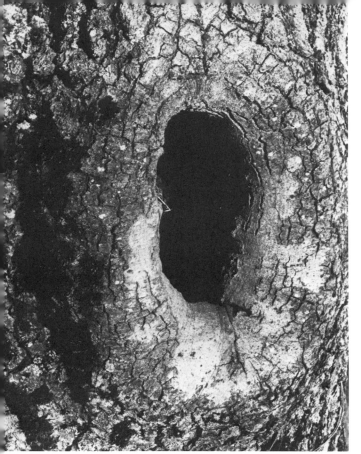

Squirrels take over tree holes.

A leaf nest

generations. But, there are usually not enough tree holes to go around for all the squirrels in a forest, so some must build outside leaf nests, also called "drays."

A leaf nest looks like a big, ragged ball, one or two feet in diameter, placed high up in a tree on a strong limb or fork near the trunk. Now, the squirrel becomes a house builder. Using its teeth, it cuts branches and twigs to the proper size. Then, with its mouth, teeth, and front feet that work like hands, it weaves the twigs and leaves together to form the foundation, sides, and roof. In the center, it makes a six-inch inner nest cavity lined with items like soft moss, dried grasses, leaves, bark, and twigs shredded with its teeth. Sometimes a squirrel works over an old crow's or hawk's nest for its house. A leaf nest is usually built by a single squirrel, although two working together have been observed.

Winter leaf nests are waterproof and rugged enough to resist high winds. Several squirrels huddle together, curled up inside the small inner nest, and stay warm and cozy. Although tree squirrels do not hibernate, they become very inactive and may remain in their nests for two or three days during severe storms.

Flying squirrels prepare their nests in exactly the same way, also preferring a vacated woodpecker hole for a den, but their house building is done at night. As many as a dozen or more flying squirrels may occupy a den during the winter.

Another kind of leaf nest, usually constructed for summer use by tree and flying squirrels, is much more loosely built and may be open at the top. This is for temporary resting on hot days. It has the disadvantage of being available to birds of prey, such as hawks or large crows, that can swoop down and snatch a snoozing squirrel. Other tree-climbing predators can also invade squirrel nests, including snakes that slither along branches, weasels, pine martens, raccoons, and owls. All leaf nests need frequent remodeling, or they fall apart.

Squirrel houses are occupied by many uninvited, unwanted guests—parasites such as fleas, mites, ticks, lice, and flies. The nests often become so infested that the animals move to cleaner quarters or build new ones. Squirrels also may suffer from mange, scabies, and several kinds of worms.

When a squirrel is running from an enemy, it may dive into a tree hole or leaf nest. Hunters report that they have heard noisy squabbles when a squirrel-on-the-run enters another's house to escape. Squirrels live in loosely organized groups and tend to be territorial, claiming feeding and property rights to certain trees and branches. The red squirrel can be especially ferocious in defending its food supply and, with loud scoldings and chatterings, will drive away any intruder that strays into its territory. Studies indicate a pecking order within groups of gray squirrels, headed

by a large adult male that is dominant in feeding and mating. Next is a number two male, and on down the line, with the older dominating the younger and males dominating females. The exception is a mother with a litter of young. She becomes aggressive and dominates everyone.

Tree squirrels begin their courtship activities in late winter and early spring with chases and skirmishes among males. The biggest,

45

During courtship, squirrels confront each other, high up in the trees.

strongest, most dominant male is accepted by the female and, after much chasing through the trees, mating occurs. She soon drives him away as she prepares a nest for her forthcoming family. She prefers a hole in a tree, lined with soft, shredded materials like

twigs, bark, bits of fur, and feathers. When she is unable to claim a tree hole, she will build an outside leaf nest. If she is a gray or fox squirrel, her three to five babies are born forty-four days after mating, thirty-eight days if she is a red squirrel, and forty days if

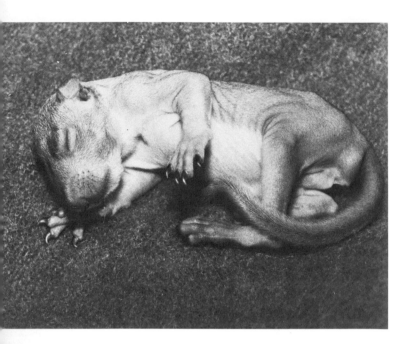

Infant tree squirrel. Note the sharp claws and long tail.

she is a flying squirrel. The infants are hairless, blind, and deaf, weighing about half an ounce, and a little over four inches in length including the tail. They come complete with all the necessary equipment for climbing—large feet with long toes and sharp claws, and an extra long tail to grow into. The mother tree squirrel takes excellent care of her young, washing them with her tongue, nursing them, and only leaving the nest when she herself must feed. If an enemy, such as a hawk or a human being, should threaten her babies, she will move them to a different nest. One at a time she carries them to the new house by grasping the loose skin on the baby's belly in her mouth, with the rest of the tiny body curled around her neck. Making her way through the trees,

48

the mother looks as though she is wearing a collar. She will fight viciously to protect her offspring from any attacker. The babies open their eyes at five to six weeks, and they begin to climb out of the den to investigate the world. By the time they are three months old, the mother may be expecting another family and will soon move to a different nest to prepare for the birth. Now the young squirrels will be on their own. Most tree squirrel species

Young gray squirrel coming out of tree hole nest.

may produce two litters during the breeding season, one in spring and another in late summer. This seems to be tied to the food supply, so when there is a large nut crop more babies are born. During times of food shortage, they may not have the second litters.

Baby squirrels have much to learn. This is a young chickaree.

The world of the trees is strange and exciting to a young squirrel, venturing out of its dark nest into daylight for the first time. There are many new sights, sounds, and smells. Instinctively, it wants to move about, for it has much to learn in a very short time. In just a few weeks the baby must master most of the skills of the grown-ups.

Some of its learning will come from rough-and-tumble play with brothers and sisters. Their games of chase, with reckless races through the treetops, give practice in escaping from predators. In play, the baby will learn to wrestle, lunge, and threaten by fluffing out its tail just as the adults do during courtship. Scolding will be practiced by teeth chattering, barking, and clucking.

It will develop other abilities such as eating new foods, nut shelling and burying, and nest building. It will begin to freeze against a limb or trunk in times of danger. And, it must heed the warning alarm calls of other squirrels and birds in the forest. All of these things are very important, because only the young squirrels that learn their lessons quickly and thoroughly will survive. Most squirrels, up to 75 percent, do not live to see their first birthdays. However, if they can get through the first year, there is a much better chance that they will be around at age two. Few live beyond five years in the wild. Only in captivity can they be expected to survive ten or more years.

Chapter 5
SQUIRREL WORLD ON THE GROUND

The squirrel must come down from its world of the trees almost every day. This is unfortunate, because the ground is a dangerous place for a tree squirrel. Away from its treetop hideaways and the safety of its nest, it has much less control over its world on the ground. Many of its main predators wait below, such as man with his guns and traps, and foxes, coyotes, bobcats, skunks, dogs, and cats.

A squirrel coming down a tree trunk is cautious and stops to look for danger before leaving the tree. When baby gray squirrels leave the nest for the first time, the mother will not allow them to go to the ground for about a week. She will push them back and scold them if they descend too soon, before they are nimble on the branches and know the familiar escape routes through the

Cats are predators. This one has just spotted an eastern gray squirrel.

foliage. Then, for their first trips down, they descend as a family so that a baby doesn't jump into the waiting jaws of a coyote or a fox.

Squirrels do much of their feeding on the ground. However, they cannot afford the luxury of hunching over their food in enjoyment, because they must be wary. A tree stump is often used as a dining table, where they can sit up high and see in all directions. A log can serve the same purpose, or they will back up to the base of a tree, which gives protection from the rear.

53

A tree stump is used as a dining table.

Acorns, right, are a favorite food.

Red squirrels store cones like these, far right, for the winter.

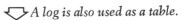 A log is also used as a table.

Tree squirrels are omnivorous, meaning that they can eat practically anything. They are limited mainly by what foods are available in the particular region where they live. Their menus also change with the season of the year. Nuts and seeds from a variety of trees are squirrel favorites: oak, hickory, elm, beech, walnut, butternut, black cherry, basswood, maple, ash, and pine. They have a sweet tooth and lap at the sap from the maple trees. In spring, strawberries prove irresistible, and they like other fruits such as wild cherry or mulberry. Mushrooms, even the kind that poison humans, and other fungi are delicacies. The buds and flowers of trees and shrubs, bark, twigs, and the farmer's corn all are favored squirrel food. They eat insects, including beetles and moths, and raid birds' nests, eating the eggs and even small birds. Squirrels consume 1½ to 2 pounds of food a week, or up to one hundred pounds a year. They also need liquid each day, which they get from fruits and berries, dew on foliage, by drinking in

Eastern gray squirrel carrying an acorn . . .

streams and ponds, and in winter by eating snow.

The phrase "squirrel away," meaning to hoard, comes from the tree squirrel's main autumn activity—the storing of large quantities of nuts in the ground for winter eating. Squirrels take this very seriously and work hard, from dawn until dusk harvesting, eating, and storing. This is the way they prepare for the food shortages of the coming winter. They do not have the cheek pouches or the underground burrows of the ground squirrels to help them carry and store food, so they use a different system. Tree squirrels, including the flying squirrels, all bury nuts in the earth for winter storage. It is interesting to watch a squirrel do

. . . and burying it . . .

. . . even deeper.

this. It begins by running along the ground with a nut in its mouth, until it finds the perfect burial place. Using its front feet, it digs a small hole a couple of inches deep and pokes the nut into the hole. It finishes the job by raking in dirt or leaves on top of the nut, giving it a few final pats with its feet. Nuts can be buried in this manner at the rate of about a nut a minute. When winter arrives and the nuts are all buried under the snow, the squirrels come down from their nests to feed. They put their sensitive noses to the ground and find the buried food by smell, not memory. They can only remember the location of a nut for about fifteen minutes after burying it. Then, they dig through the snow, often going down several feet to get an acorn.

It takes considerable skill to eat a hard nut. The squirrel sits back on its haunches in what is called the "squirrel stance" or crouch, holding the nut in its forepaws. It rotates the nut between its palms, gnawing through the hard shell with its two lower front teeth, using the upper teeth as supports, until there is a round hole. When the hole is large enough for the lower teeth to fit inside, they break open the nut. The squirrel has four razor-sharp front incisor teeth, two above and two below, that keep growing throughout its lifetime. It must keep filing these off by gnawing on hard objects, such as nuts and tree bark, or they become so long that the animal cannot eat. Gray, tassel-eared, and flying squirrels have a total of twenty-two teeth, and the red and fox squirrels have twenty.

Members of the red squirrel family living in evergreen forests use a different method of food storage. Their autumn food is mostly the seeds or tiny nuts located under the scales of the cones on pine, fir, and spruce trees. The squirrels pile up a large number of cones in one place, called a cache. When the snow comes, they only have to find a cache of cones, instead of having to nose out each individual nut like the other tree squirrels. The chickarees begin harvesting the cones while they are still green and sticky with pitch. They clip them off with their teeth, often from a height of one hundred or more feet in the treetops. Some of these cones can be very large, such as those on the Jeffrey pine that weigh up to five pounds, considerably more than the eight-ounce squirrel. The animal then descends the tree and either carries or drags the cones to a secluded place under a log or at the base of a tree, usually close to its nest tree. It may collect hundreds of small cones in a cache and make several caches in different locations. When winter comes and the cones are covered by snow, the squirrel uses its strong sense of smell to find them. It tunnels under the snow, popping up its head through openings every several feet to look around. Reaching the cache, it has a feast.

Eating on a pinecone is different from an acorn. Holding the

cone in its front paws, the squirrel strips off the scales with its
front teeth and eats the seeds inside. When it is finished, the cone
looks like a roasting ear of brown corn with every kernel removed. Red squirrels also bury individual nuts and seeds, just as
the other tree squirrels do.

Chickaree eating on a large pinecone.
◁

When a squirrel has finished eating, a cone looks like an ear of corn with every kernel removed. ▷

As they squirrel away their food, tree squirrels also keep eating so that they can go into winter with extra fat on their bodies. By then, they also have shed their fur, or molted, and have new, heavier coats to help them stay warm. Squirrels molt twice a year, in spring and fall.

What happens when gray and red squirrels live in the same territory and compete for food? Who wins?

I observed this situation in a dense forest of very tall fir trees. A chickaree climbed at least one hundred feet into a tree and cut loose a huge cone weighing several pounds. It crashed to the ground with a loud thud. A large gray squirrel, sitting nearby, leisurely walked over to the cone and started to strip scales and eat the seeds. The chickaree came racing down the trunk headfirst

Gray squirrel with pitch
around its mouth.

to claim its treasure, stopping when it spotted the gray. It clung to the side of the tree surveying the scene. Now, what did it do? Attack? No, it began to chatter with a clucking, *churr-ring* sound. Finally, it ascended and stood a few yards away from the busy gray, its small body trembling all over, and scolded. It sputtered and clucked in a shrill, loud voice, but it didn't get any closer. The gray kept on eating, paying no attention. Finally, the chickaree ran back up into the tree, harvested another cone, and this time salvaged its prize.

Tree squirrels do not have serious fights, even over food. On another occasion, three red squirrels wanted the same cone. One was gnawing at the stem end, when another raced toward it. The first squirrel squeaked and dashed away, and the second took over. The first stayed nearby, chattering its teeth. Suddenly, a third squirrel jumped at the new owner, quietly eating, and drove it off in the same way. There was much growling and squeaking by both displaced squirrels, but the third one had apparently taken command. This was especially interesting because the ground was littered with juicy, pitch-filled cones, and yet all wanted the same one.

Two gray squirrels had a similar skirmish over an acorn, which involved nothing more than a running threat, with one making a quick pass at the other amid barking and chattering. This time

63

the original owner didn't give up its acorn and drove off the intruder.

Tree squirrels become very familiar with their world on the ground and use the same routes over and over, just as they do in the trees. When danger threatens, they can run surprisingly fast, up to seventeen miles an hour, with bounds that cover five to six feet.

Perhaps it is a good thing that squirrels store their food in the ground instead of in the trees where they would be safer. At least it is better for mankind, because squirrels are great foresters. They are responsible for the growth of many trees in our woodlands. Every year they bury millions of nuts and seeds, more than they can possibly use. Many of these are never recovered and go on to germinate and sprout into new trees, helping to reforest our land.

Chapter 6
SQUIRRELS ON THE MOVE

The most amazing tree squirrel stories have to do with "squirrel migrations." Although squirrels rarely venture more than two to three hundred feet from their nest trees, every so often something mysterious happens to make them move. Huge numbers suddenly leave their home territories—for somewhere else, far away.

It usually occurs in the fall of the year. Thousands of squirrels all at once set out from the forest, crossing cleared fields, farm lands, highways, and even mountains. Ordinarily, squirrels avoid swimming, but during these migrations they often take to the water, swimming across whatever is in the way. Many of the swimmers become exhausted and drown.

Earliest reports of squirrel movements date to 1749 and 1780,

Most of the migrations have been by eastern gray squirrels. ⌂

◁ *Tree squirrels live in high places. They rarely leave their home areas.*

when masses of squirrels were on the move in Pennsylvania and Kentucky. Several major migrations were reported in the early 1800s in Vermont, New York, and Ohio, and large numbers of squirrels were seen swimming in the Hudson, Niagara, and Ohio rivers. But none of these equaled the migration of a half billion gray squirrels that occurred in southern Wisconsin in the fall of 1842. It lasted four weeks, and observers stated that it looked like an advancing army, 150 miles long and 130 miles wide.

In this century, there have been smaller migrations in the eastern United States and New England, as well as in Minnesota,

Missouri, and Arkansas. Although most of these involved only the gray squirrel, a 1946 movement of gray and fox squirrels was reported in northwestern Wisconsin. Both species were observed swimming in rivers, crossing roads, and invading cornfields.

The most recent extensive migration was in September of 1968. It is estimated that about 20 million gray squirrels were on the move in most of the eastern states from Vermont to Georgia. They appeared in all kinds of unlikely places, such as in people's gardens, on golf courses, and in farmers' fields, with thousands killed on the highways. They tried to swim across lakes and rivers, and squirrel bodies littered the banks of the Hudson River. Fifty-five tons of dead squirrels were removed from a New York reservoir. In recent years, there have been several smaller squirrel migrations, so apparently it can happen any time.

The question that remains unanswered is, *why?* What caused these millions of squirrels to leave their tree homes and start moving, many facing certain disaster. No one really knows for sure, but scientists have collected some facts about these movements.

For one thing, they tended to occur when squirrel populations were very high. The nut crops were especially plentiful the year or two before the movement but were currently poor. The travelers were usually plump and healthy and not abnormally in-

fested with parasites. In the 1968 migration, most of the animals were young, born in the previous spring. So, what does all of this mean?

One guess is that squirrel migration is nature's way of solving the problems of overcrowding and getting rid of excess numbers. Young squirrels move into new regions, spreading out the population, with many eliminated on the way.

Many mysteries remain. Dr. Vagn Flyger, a University of Maryland biologist and an authority on squirrel migration, has been studying the problem for years and hopes eventually to find the answers to puzzling questions. Why do migrating squirrels all seem to be going the same way? How many squirrels in a population take part? How fast do they travel? How far do they go? Do any of the squirrels return?

Some day the puzzle may be solved.

Chapter 7
TREE SQUIRRELS
AND MAN

The tree squirrel's greatest problem is man. This may seem surprising, since it is one of the few wild animals willing to share its existence with humans. In parks throughout the country, tree squirrels share in man's picnics, band concerts, and Sunday strolls, and accept his food scraps and peanuts.

But it is man that has destroyed much of the squirrel's habitat by cutting down forests to plant crops and build houses, eliminating its food supply and nest sites. Man's guns kill millions every year for sport, food, and fur, and his automobiles slaughter many on the highways.

The fox squirrel has especially suffered. As the oak, hickory, and other hardwood trees were felled in New England and the northeastern United States, the species completely disappeared in

71

The fox squirrel has especially suffered loss of habitat. ⇨

Drinking from a fountain, this squirrel has learned to adapt to man's world. ⇦

⇩ *Fallen trees destroy squirrel nests.*

many areas. An effort is being made by the United States Fish and Wildlife Service to recover one subspecies, the Delmarva Peninsula fox squirrel, and restore it to its original range that once stretched from New Jersey, through Pennsylvania, Delaware, Maryland, and Virginia. Today it exists mainly on two wildlife refuges in Maryland and in one Virginia location. So what can be done to save a squirrel? The recovery plan involves preserving and providing food and nests for the fox squirrels and protecting them from hunters, poachers, and predators. It includes moving some animals into new areas and promoting the program to gain public support. An important part of the project has to do with assuring adequate nests by protecting nest trees and, when necessary, providing nest boxes.

Nest boxes are usually made of wood, about ten inches high, ten inches wide, and fifteen inches long, with a two-inch opening near the top for an entrance. They are placed fifteen to twenty feet above the ground in trees, to be used as dens by the squirrels. Where they have been provided, in some parks and forests, squirrels have seemed to prefer them to their own nests and have moved in immediately. Studies show that the use of nest boxes will double a squirrel population in an area and are a way that humans can help squirrels. They are also valuable in squirrel research for capturing and marking animals.

Do squirrels make good pets? The answer is probably "no," unless you don't mind a pet that runs up and down drapes and curtains, jumps onto lampshades, chews up furniture, and climbs people, often balancing on human heads or shoulders. Squirrels are excitable and undependable and tend to bite. Like other wild animals, they should remain in their natural habitat. However, occasionally someone finds a newborn squirrel fallen from a nest and ends up trying to raise it. What a challenge! The infant must be fed warm milk every four hours, day and night. And, if the

Newborn squirrels must be fed every four hours around the clock.

baby survives infancy and becomes tame, it should never be released back into the wild. It will have lost its distrust of man and may be killed by hunters, as well as by dogs and cats. It is said that a human-reared squirrel can't last a day in the forest and will be attacked and harassed by other squirrels when it enters their territories.

No two squirrels are exactly alike. Just like humans, each one is different. There are some examples of exceptional squirrels that have gotten along very well in the domestic world. A gray squirrel in Florida, named Twiggy, was taught to water-ski behind a toy boat and learned to perform at shows. A troupe of six tame

squirrels toured Europe as entertainers, doing tricks like playing dead, trapeze performing, turning somersaults, and tightrope walking. Some say that flying squirrels are trainable, if you aren't bothered by their gliding around all night while you are asleep.

Not everyone appreciates tree squirrels, because they can cause trouble. In cities, they sometimes gnaw into electrical cables, wires, and transformers, causing unpopular power failures. A wild

*Fox squirrel stripping bark
from a tree branch.*

squirrel in an unoccupied attic or basement can do great damage. When squirrels strip bark from trees, the trees may die, making forestry officials unhappy. And, when squirrels migrate across farm lands, they ruin crops, causing farmers to be unhappy. Some of the loudest objections come from people who want to feed the birds without feeding the squirrels. They frequently complain that the crafty squirrels can outmaneuver practically any "squirrel-proof" bird feeder. There are many stories of daring feats accomplished by acrobatic squirrels to invade feeders, and the squirrels usually win!

All of these misdeeds reflect the squirrel's big problem of living in man's territory and coming into conflict with him. When squirrels get into trouble, they aren't being bad. They are just being squirrels—very special little wild animals trying to adapt to the human world.

INDEX